Visual Basic 2010

CODING BRIEFS

DATA ACCESS

KEVIN HOUGH

DALLAS, TX, USA

VISUAL BASIC 2010

CODING BRIEFS

DATA ACCESS

© 2011 Runtime Publishing, LLC

For information on obtaining written permission for the use of material from this publication, please submit a written request to:

Runtime Publishing, LLC
14902 Preston Rd, Suite 404-505
Dallas, TX 75254-5434

The author and the publisher have made every effort in the publication of this book to ensure the accuracy of the content. The content in this book is sold without warranty, either expressed or implied.

ISBN 978-0-9836151-6-3

1st Printing, July 2011

To my wife, Cheryl, for all of her support, encouragement, and love.

Table of Contents

CODING BRIEFS

Runtime Publishing's Coding Briefs series uses a practical, step-by-step approach that has been specially designed to guide you, the developer, through a complete development project and solution in each and every volume.

Several times per year, a new volume of **Coding Briefs,** discussing a new and exciting development topic, is published in an 8.5" x 11" full-color format and traditional black and white format for easy reading, and easy access is provided for downloading the volume's complete code and examples.

Coding Briefs, from Runtime Publishing LLC, are offered in Visual Basic and C# formats, and are available in print, on-line, and as eBooks.

JOIN US A
OUR WEB SIT

**Visit Runtime Publishing
http://www.runtimepublishing.cc
for all sorts of information about c
publications.**

ABOUT THE AUTHOR

Kevin Hough heads the Project Management Office and the Software Engineering department at Trans-Trade, Inc in Dallas, TX, USA.

He has been developing enterprise level software since 1983 and has specialized in Microsoft technologies since 1990. Currently, he is developing with Visual Basic, C#, SQL Server, Silverlight, and Dot-NetNuke.

Kevin has designed and developed large scale commercial applications and Web sites for corporations including EXXON, Pennzoil, Compaq, Shell, and Texaco, as well as for leading universities, including Harvard, Stanford, and Rice. You can reach Kevin at kevinh@runtimepublishing.com.

The Audience for Coding Briefs

Visual Basic 2010 Coding Briefs Data Access is written for the intermediate level developer. To get the most out of this book, the developer should be familiar with the following tasks:

- Creating solutions in Visual Studio 2010

- Developing code in Visual Basic 2010

- Writing If/Then/Else statements

- Creating and calling Functions and Procedures

- Working with My.Settings to store Strings

- Debugging code

- Working with Stored Procedures

Obtaining the Code

The source code is included in the project files that can be downloaded from www.runtimepublishing.com. Follow these steps to get the code up and running:

1. Follow the steps in the section, *Quick Start,* to register and unlock the code for this Coding Brief
2. Enter the Unlock Code that is located in the section *Running the Windows Sample Application* later in this brief
3. Open the projects in Visual Studio 2010.

The code for this brief includes the following projects:

Project	Description
CBDaraAccess	Data Access framework
CodingBriefsVolume1	Windows WinForms application
CodingBriefsVolume1Web	ASP .Net based Web application

VISUAL BASIC 2010
Coding Briefs
DATA ACCESS

In today's high-tech, information driven world, the security of personal data is vital. We have all heard the horror stories of personal data being compromised from companies, both large and small.

The data access framework that we will develop in Coding Briefs will allow us to create datasets, execute queries, and select data in a secure, managed process.

This framework will provide a solid foundation for managing secure data access through stored procedures, allowing us to select, insert, update, and delete records from a SQL Server database. We will have access to parameterized queries and will develop an automated process for discovering stored procedure parameters.

The major areas that we will address in this brief are as follows:

- Discussing the Data Access Framework (DAL)
- Managing the Database Connections
- Selecting Records
- Manipulating Data
- Preparing the Select and Execute Methods
- Working with Parameters
- Testing the Data Access Framework

And, as a bonus, two complete sample applications have been added; one for Windows, and one in ASP .Net, that will test all of the features on the data access framework.

Defining the Data Access Framework

The data access framework in this brief needs to be able to store and retrieve all of the data that is necessary for our data centric applications to perform as they are designed to. In order to accomplish this data access task, we will rely on the following tools and practices:

- All of the data for Coding Briefs will be stored in a SQL Server 2008 database

- All of the business rules will be managed in a series of Business Object classes

- We will have a central data access layer (DAL) that can be called from any form, class, or module in Windows and ASPX applications

- All database interaction will employ stored procedures

With the Microsoft tools that are available to us, and a little ingenuity, we can design and develop a very robust Data Access Framework that can be used, not only for Coding Briefs, but for most other applications that we develop in the future

In the next section, we design the data access framework.

Designing the Data Access Framework

For a data access framework to be useful and effective, it must be easy for the developer to use, and flexible enough to accommodate all types of data access requests. The data access framework in Coding Briefs solves both those important issues.

Figure 1: Basic Data Access Flow, as shown below, depicts the basic flow of the data access framework.

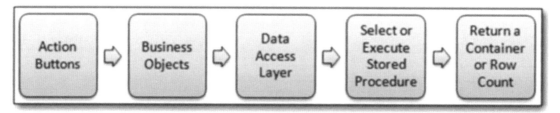

Figure 1: Basic Data Access Flow

The DAL of Coding Briefs Data Access Framework is designed to perform two major tasks:

- Select records

- Execute actions against records

Selecting Records

A well designed DAL will allow the developer to select records and return them in a container, such as a DataSet, or a SqlDataReader. The DAL that we will develop for Coding Briefs is no exception. It will allow us to select records and return the selection as a DataSet or a SqlDataReader.

Executing Records

Coding Briefs' DAL provides functionality to execute an action type stored procedure. Action stored procedures are those that insert records, update records, or delete records from a database. For execution, the number of affected rows is returned. So now that we have a high-level view of the functionality of the DAL, it is time to jump in and get started developing it.

In the next section, we will get the sample applications up and running.

Quick Start Guide

We are ready to get the project running. And, we are in luck. This volume of Coding Briefs includes the fully developed data access framework, as well as, two sample applications; one for Windows and one for ASP .NET.

Running the Sample Applications

Follow these steps to get the Windows Sample Application (WSA) up and running:

1. Register for an account at www.runtimepublishing.com

2. Log into the site

3. Click the Register Publication menu option

4. Select the publication name from the dropdown

5. Enter the Unlock Code that is located in the section, *Running the Windows Sample Application,* later on in this brief

6. Click the Submit link to register your copy of Coding Briefs

7. Click on the Subscribers Lounge menu option

8. Select the edition of the publication that has been registered (Example: Visual Basic Coding Briefs for eBooks, or C# Coding Briefs Online, etc)

9. Click on the Download Code link for your volume and save the Zip file to a location on your local hard drive

10. Unzip the file and see all the projects that are available for your publication

11. Follow the steps in the section, *Attaching the Contact Database,* to attach the database

12. Open the Windows sample and the ASP .Net sample projects

13. Select Project → Coding Briefs volume Properties to open the Property Pages

14. Select the Settings tab and check the cbConn Connection String to make sure that it is setup properly for your server, then make any changes that are necessary

When you're ready, press F5 to start the Windows Sample Application, as shown in Figure 2.

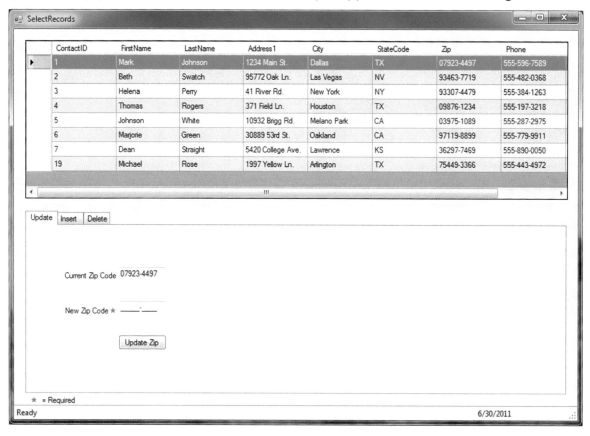

Figure 2: The Windows Sample Application

Managing the Database Connections

In order to manage the database connections, we must be able to make a connection to the database, and to disconnect from the database.

In Coding Briefs, we don't want to keep a persistent connection to the database. Instead, we want to open the database, perform our select or execute action, and then close the database.

Opening a Database Connection

To perform an action against the database, we have to open a connection to the database. When we open a database connection, we can access the objects of the database by making calls to the open database.

The following code, shown in Listing 1, is used to open a database connection.

```
Public Sub DBConnect(
  ByVal connectionString As String,
  ByRef errorParms() As Object)

  Try
    SqlConn = New SqlConnection(connectionString)
      SqlConn.Open()
  Catch
    ' Return the error to the calling program.
    errorParms(0) = 999
    errorParms(1) = Err.Description
    errorParms(2) =
        System.Reflection.MethodBase.
        GetCurrentMethod.Name
  End Try
End Sub
```

Listing 1: Opening a Database Connection

The code shown in Listing 1 opens a connection to the database.

The procedure DBConnect accepts one parameter, the connection string, and thereby allows us to open different databases based on the connection string that is passed to DBConnect.

A SqlConnection object represents a unique session to a SQL Server data source, and it is used together with a SqlDataAdapter and a SqlCommand to increase performance when connecting to a Microsoft SQL Server database.

- First, we set the variable SQLConn to a SQLConnection, and use the connection string that is passed to the procedure
- Next, we open the connection with the Open command

In the next section, we will discuss the process and the code necessary to close a database connection.

Closing Connections

When a SqlConnection goes out of scope, it won't be closed, so we have to explicitly close the connection by calling Close or Dispose. Close and Dispose will both close a connection to an open database; however, Close is the preferred method of closing any open connection.

The code shown below in Listing 2 can be used to close a database connection.

```vb
Public Sub DBDisconnect(ByRef errorParms As Object)

   Try
      SqlConn.Close()
      SqlConn = Nothing
      SqlCmd = Nothing
   Catch
      ' Return the error to the calling program.
      errorParms(0) = 999
      errorParms(1) = Err.Description
      errorParms(2) =
         System.Reflection.MethodBase.
               GetCurrentMethod.Name
   End Try
End Sub
```

Listing 2: Closing a Database Connection

The code in Listing 2 closes the database connection and sets the connection and the command objects to nothing, therefore, releasing the resources. Managing database connections is an important part of a good data access framework.

In the next section, we will develop the code that we will use to select records in Coding Briefs.

Selecting Records

The Data Access Framework that we are developing for this brief will provide functionality to select records and to execute actions against records. In this section, we will focus our attention on selecting records and returning either a DataSet or a SQLDataReader.

Creating a DataSet Class

A DataSet class represents data that is cached in memory, and it is a major component in ADO.NET architecture and in Coding Briefs' data access framework. A Dataset consists of a collection of DataTables.

The code in Listing 3 is used to create a dataset and return it to the calling procedure.

```vb
Public Function DBCreateDataset(
  ByVal SPName As String,
  ByVal cbConn As String,
  ByRef errorParms() As Object, Optional
  ByRef parms() As Object = Nothing
  ) As DataSet

  Dim dsResult As New DataSet
  Dim i As Int16 = 0
  Dim j As Int16 = 0
  Dim numOutParms As Int16 = 0

  Try ' Open the connection, create the
    Command, add values to the parameters.
    Call SetUpSP(SPName, numOutParms,
    cbConn, errorParms, parms)
    ' If there was an errors, exit
    If errorParms(0) = 999 Then
      Return Nothing
      Exit Function
    End If


    ' Execute the Stored
    SqlDA = New SqlDataAdapter(SqlCmd)
    DBCreateDataset = New DataSet
    DBCreateDataset = dsResult
    SqlDA.Fill(dsResult)

    ' If the SP has Output parms,
    ' set them up to be returned.
    If numOutParms > 0 Then
      i = SetOutParms(parms,
      numOutParms, errorParms)
    End If

    ' If there was an exit.
    If errorParms(0) = 999 Then
      Return Nothing
      Exit Function
    End If

    ' Close the connection and clear the Cmd
    If SqlConn.State = ConnectionState.Open Then
      Call Me.DBDisconnect(errorParms)
      ' If there was an error, exit.
      If errorParms(0) = 999 Then
        Return Nothing
        Exit Function
      End If
    End If
  Catch
    ' Return the error to the calling program.
    errorParms(0) = 999
    errorParms(1) = Err.Description
    errorParms(2) = System.Reflection.MethodBase
    .GetCurrentMethod.Name
  End Try
  ' Return the DataSet
  Return dsResult
End Function
```

Listing 3: Creating a Dataset

The code shown in Listing 3 creates a DataSet and returns it to the calling procedure, where it can be evaluated and used.

The first part of Listing 3 calls the SetUpSP procedure that we will develop later in this Coding Brief. SetUpSP opens the connection to the database, creates the SQLCommand object, and adds values to the parameters.

The second part of the code sets up the SqlDataAdapter, creates the empty DataSet, and uses the SqlDataAdapter to fill the DataSet.

A SqlDataAdapter serves as a bridge between a DataSet and SQL Server, and can be used for retrieving and saving data. SqlDataAdapter provides this bridge by mapping the Fill function, which changes the data in the DataSet to match the data in the data source from the SQLCommand object.

The next code section creates the Output parameters, if there are any. Notice in the definition of the DBCreateDataSet procedure that parms is declared as ByRef. Variables that are declared as ByRef can be changed by the calling program. In this case, we will change the parms variable to hold any Output parameters that the stored procedure returns and they will be available to the calling program in the parms variable.

The Catch statement has error trapping. That will display the description of the error, and the location of the error in the code base.

The last part of the code returns the dsResult DataSet to the calling procedure.

Returning a SqlDataReader Class

In the previous section, we created a DataSet, a cache of data from the commands in a stored procedure. There are other ways to retrieve data, and we will rely on the SqlDataReader class to return data in this brief, as well as DataSets.

A SqlDataReader class provides a way of reading a forward-only stream of rows from a SQL Server database. An advantage of using a SqlDataReader class is that it is very lightweight. It is a great way to see if a SELECT statement returns any rows. It can be used in cases such as verifying a user's login credentials, or to populate lists, as shown in Listing 4.

```
Public Function DBGetSqlDataReader _
  (ByVal spName As String,
  ByVal cbConn As String,
  ByRef errorParms() As Object, Optional _
  ByRef parms() As Object = Nothing) As
SqlDataReader

  Dim DBdataReader As SqlDataReader =
  Nothing
  Dim rowCnt As Int16 = 0
  Dim i As Int16 = 0
  Dim numOutParms As Int16 = 0
  Try ' Open the connection, create the
  Command, add values to the parameters.
    Call SetUpSP(spName, numOutParms,
      cbConn, errorParms, parms)
    ' If there was an error, exit.
    If errorParms(0) = 999 Then
      Return Nothing
      Exit Function
    End If
    ' Execute the SP and return a DataReader.
    DBdataReader = SqlCmd.ExecuteReader()
    'If the SP has Output parms,
    'set them up to be returned.
    If nOurms > 0 Then
      i = SetOutParms(parms,
      numOutParms, errorParms)
    End If


    ' If there was an error, exit
    If errorParms(0) = 999 Then
      Return Nothing
      Exit Function
    End If
  Catch ' Return the error
    errorParms(0) = 999
    errorParms(1) = Err.Description
    errorParms(2) = System.Reflection.
      MethodBase.GetCurrentMethod.Name
  End Try
  Return DBdataReader
End Function
```

Listing 4: Returning a SQLDataReader

The code in Listing 4 creates a SqlDataReader and returns it to the calling procedure.

The first part of the code in Listing 4 calls the SetUpSP procedure that we will develop later in this brief. SetUpSP opens the connection to the database, creates the SQLCommand object, and adds values to the parameters.

The second part of the code calls the ExecuteReader method, which sends the CommandText to the Connection and builds a SqlDataReader.

The next code section creates the Output parameters, if there are any. Notice in the definition of the DBCreateDataSet procedure that parms is declared as ByRef. Variables that are declared as ByRef can be changed by the calling program. In this case, we will change the parms variable to hold any Output parameters that the stored procedure returns, and they will be available to the calling program in the parms variable.

The Catch statement has our normal error trapping.

The last part of the code returns the SqlDataReader to the calling procedure.

The DataSet and the SqlDataReader are two of the most useful ways to select and return data.

In the next section, we will develop the code that will be used in Coding Briefs to execute actions against data.

Manipulating Data

Manipulating data by executing actions such as insert, update, and delete are normal in a data driven applications.

There are several types of action commands, including the following:

- Create, which creates a database object, such as a database itself, a table, or a function
- Delete, which deletes a row or an object from a database
- Insert, which inserts a new row into a table
- Update, which updates the data in a row, or a set of row

Table 1 summarizes the commands that are available in SQL Server 2008 to manipulate data.

TABLE 1: Data Manipulation Commands

Item	Description
BeginExecuteNon-Query	Initiates the asynchronous execution of a Transact-SQL statement or stored procedure that is described by the SqlCommand. The INSERT, DELETE, UPDATE, and SET statements are usually executed.
BeginExecuteReader	Starts the asynchronous execution of a Transact-SQL statement or stored procedure that is described by the SqlCommand. One or more results sets from the server are returned.
BeginExecuteXmlReader	Starts the execution of the Transact-SQL statement or stored procedure asynchronously that is described by the SqlCommand.
ExecuteReader	Executes commands that return rows.
ExecuteNonQuery	Executes Transact-SQL commands such as INSERT, DELETE, UPDATE, and SET statements.
ExecuteScalar	Retrieves a single value (for example, an aggregate value) from a database.
ExecuteXmlReader	Sends the CommandText to the Connection and builds an XmlReader object.

In today's enterprise, data is everywhere and our users want it. They want to create new data, and have the ability to delete data, and/or change data. As developers, we must be able to combine all of the action commands that are at our disposal and make them work in concert, like a well tuned orchestra.

We must make sure that a delete command is restrictive enough to protect vital data, while being agile enough to fulfill our users' needs. When we deal with complex data, this can be very challenging.

With all of the data that is at our fingertips, we must see to it that we don't have butter fingers! And, it is up to us to utilize all of the tools we have to provide the users the data that they want, when they want it, and how they want it.

In the next section, we will create the code necessary to execute a transact SQL statement against a data connection using the ExecuteNonQuery command.

Executing Transact-SQL Commands

Executing Transact-SQL Commands to manipulate data is a major part of any data centric application. In the normal course of business, we need to be able to create new objects, delete existing date, insert new data, and update existing data. We can achieve all of this by creating a custom procedure to perform the ExecuteNonQuery Sql Command, as shown in Listing 5.

```vbnet
Public Function DBExecNonQuery _
  (ByVal spName As String,
  ByVal cbConn As String,
  ByRef errorParms As Object, Optional _
  ByRef parms() As Object = Nothing) As Integer

  Dim rowCnt As Int16 = 0
  Dim i As Int16 = 0
  Dim j As Int16 = 0
  Dim numOutParms As Int16 = 0
  Try
    ' Open the connection, create the Command, and
    ' add values to the parameters.
    Call SetUpSP(spName, numOutParms,
    cbConn, errorParms, parms)

    ' If there was an error, exit
    If errorParms(0) = 999 Then
      Return Nothing
      Exit Function
    End If
    ' Execute the Stored Procedure
    rowCnt = SqlCmd.ExecuteNonQuery()
    'If the SP has Output parms,
    'set them up to be returned.
    If numOutParms > 0 Then
      i = SetOutParms(parms, numOutParms,
      errorParms)
    End If
    ' If there was an error, exit.
    If errorParms(0) = 999 Then
      Return Nothing
      Exit Function
    End If
    'Close the connection and clear the Cmd Object
    If SqlConn.State = ConnectionState.Open Then
      Call Me.DBDisconnect(errorParms)
      ' If there was an error, exit
      If errorParms(0) = 999 Then
        Return Nothing
        Exit Function
      End If
    End If
    'Return the ReturnValue or the row count
    If rowCnt = -1 Then
      Return SqlCmd.Parameters(0).Value
    Else
      Return rowCnt
    End If
  Catch ' Return the error to the calling program.
    errorParms(0) = 999
    errorParms(1) = Err.Description
    errorParms(2) = System.Reflection.MethodBase.
      GetCurrentMethod.Name
    DBExecNonQuery = Nothing
  End Try
End Function
```

Listing 5: Executing Transact-SQL Commands

The code in Listing 5 performs the ExecuteNonQuery method to manipulate data.

The first part of the code calls the SetUpSP procedure, which is common to both the select and execute procedures that we will develop later in this brief. SetUpSP opens the connection to the database, creates the SQLCommand object, and adds values to the parameters.

The second part of the code calls the ExecuteNonQuery method, which executes the Transact-SQL statements and returns the number of rows affected.

The next code section creates the Output parameters, if there are any. Notice in the definition of the DBCreateDataSet procedure that parms is declared as ByRef. Variables that are declared as ByRef can be changed by the calling program. In this case, we will change the parms variable to hold any Output parameters that the stored procedure returns and they will be available to the calling program in the parms variable.

The next part of the code returns the row count to the calling procedure. If the ExecuteNon-Query method selects rows, it will return -1 as the row count. If the ExecuteNonQuery method performs an action against the database, it will return the number of rows affected.

The Catch statement has our normal error trapping. If an error is encountered, it will be returned to the calling program.

The ExecuteNonQuery method is one of the most versatile methods available to us for manipulating data.

In the next section, we will look at stored procedures and how to create them.

Working with Stored Procedures

Stored procedures consist of a group of Structured Query Language statements that are named and stored in the database in compiled form, thus allowing them to be shared by any number of applications. Stored procedures have the following advantages over using in-line SQL statements:

- Help in controlling access to the data
- Allow select and execute statements to be changed without having to recompile the application that uses them
- Provide uniform access to data
- Can be reused without having to recreate the code
- Provide access to database objects that are both secure and uniform
- Provide reduced development cost and increased reliability

Examining the Anatomy of a Stored Procedure

Stored procedures are pre-compiled groups of SQL statements that select data or perform some type of action on data. The syntax of a stored procedure is displayed in Code 1.

```
CREATE { PROC | PROCEDURE } [schema_name.] procedure_name
[ ; number ]
  [ { @parameter [ type_schema_name. ] data_type }
    [ VARYING ] [ = default ] [ OUT | OUTPUT ] [READONLY]
  ] [ ,...n ]
[ WITH <procedure_option> [ ,...n ] ]
[ FOR REPLICATION ]
AS { <sql_statement> [;][ ...n ] | <method_specifier> };]
<procedure_option> ::=
  [ ENCRYPTION ]
  [ RECOMPILE ]
  [ EXECUTE AS Clause ]
<sql_statement> ::=
{ [ BEGIN ] statements [ END ] }
<method_specifier> ::=
EXTERNAL NAME assembly_name.class_name.method_name
```

Code 1: Stored Procedure Syntax

Tools for Creating Stored Procedures

There are two main ways to create stored procedures; you can use Visual Studio 2010, or the SQL Server 2008 Management Studio (SSMS).

Table 2: Stored Procedure Arguments

Argument	Description
schema_name	The name of the schema to which the procedure belongs
procedure_name	The name of the new stored procedure. Procedure names must comply with the rules for identifiers and must be unique within the schema
; number	An optional integer that is used to group procedures of the same name
@ parameter	A parameter in the procedure. . The value of each declared parameter must be supplied by the calling program unless a default for the parameter is defined or the value is set to equal another parameter
[type_schema_name.] data_type	The data type of the parameter and the schema to which it belongs
VARYING	Specifies the result set supported as an output parameter
default	A default value for the parameter
OUTPUT	Indicates that the parameter is an output parameter that will return a value to the calling program.
READONLY	Indicates that the parameter cannot be updated or modified within the body of the procedure.
RECOMPILE	Indicates that the Database Engine does not cache a plan for this procedure and the procedure is compiled at run time
ENCRYPTION	Indicates that SQL Server will encrypt the original text of the CREATE PROCEDURE statement
EXECUTE AS	Specifies the security context under which to execute the stored procedure
FOR REPLICATION	Specifies that stored procedures that are created for replication cannot be executed on the Subscriber
<sql_statement>	One or more Transact-SQL statements that make up the procedure
EXTERNAL NAME	Specifies the method of a .NET Framework assembly for a CLR stored procedure to reference

Creating Stored Procedures in Visual Studio 2010

This is a good time to acquaint ourselves with the tools that are available for creating stored procedures from within the Visual Studio 2010 IDE. Follow these steps to create a stored procedure from within the Visual Studio 2010 IDE:

1. Select View —>Server Explorer to add the Server Explorer window to the IDE, as shown in Figure 3

2. Click on the Connect to Database Connection icon 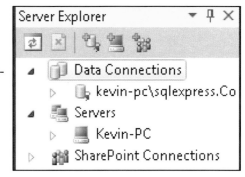 , or right mouse click on Data Connections to open the Add Connection dialog box as shown in Figure 4

3. Enter your server name. If you are using SQL Server Express, you can use .\sqlexpress as the server name

4. Select CodingBriefs from the list of databases

5. Click the OK button to add the data connection

6. Expand the database node in the Server Explorer window

Figure 3: Server Explorer

7. Right mouse click on the Stored Procedures folder and select Add New Stored Procedure to open a new blank stored procedure window, as shown in Figure 5

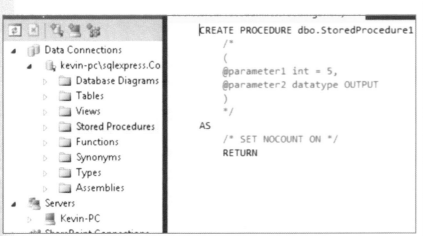

Figure 5: Stored Procedure Window

From this new window in Figure 5, we can create our new stored procedures.

So, now that we know the basics of creating stored procedures from within Visual Studio 2010, let's turn our attention to using the SSMS.

Figure 4: Add Connection Dialog Box

Creating Stored Procedures in the SSMS

The SSMS is a great tool for developers to use for creating and managing stored procedures. It is flexible, easy to use, and easy to customize.

Follow these steps to create a new stored procedure in the SSMS:

1. Open the SSMS if it is not already open
2. Expand the list of databases
3. Expand the CodingBriefs database
4. Right mouse click on the stored procedures folder and select New Stored Procedure to open the Stored Procedure template in a new window, as shown below

```
-- =============================================
-- Template generated from Template Explorer using:
-- Create Procedure (New Menu).SQL
--
-- Use the Specify Values for Template Parameters
-- command (Ctrl-Shift-M) to fill in the parameter
-- values below.
--
-- This block of comments will not be included in
-- the definition of the procedure.
-- =============================================
SET ANSI_NULLS ON
GO
SET QUOTED_IDENTIFIER ON
GO
-- =============================================
-- Author:      <Author,,Name>
-- Create date: <Create Date,,>
-- Description: <Description,,>
-- =============================================
CREATE PROCEDURE <Procedure_Name, sysname, ProcedureName>
    -- Add the parameters for the stored procedure here
    <@Param1, sysname, @p1> <Datatype_For_Param1 >,
    <@Param2, sysname, @p2> <Datatype_For_Param2 >
AS
BEGIN
    -- SET NOCOUNT ON added to prevent extra result sets from
    -- interfering with SELECT statements.
    SET NOCOUNT ON;

    -- Insert statements for procedure here
    SELECT <@Param1, sysname, @p1>, <@Param2, sysname, @p2>
END
GO
```

The stored procedure template is divided into 5 sections. The sections are as follows:

1. The Template description at the top of the stored procedure

2. The second section sets ANSI_NULLS and QUOTED_IDENTIFIER on

    a. When SET ANSI_NULLS is ON, a SELECT statement that uses WHERE column_name = NULL returns zero rows even if there are null values in column_name. A SELECT statement that uses WHERE column_name <> NULL returns zero rows even if there are nonnull values in column_name.

    b. When SET QUOTED_IDENTIFIER is ON, identifiers can be delimited by double quotation marks, and literals must be delimited by single quotation marks. When SET QUOTED_IDENTIFIER is OFF, identifiers cannot be quoted and must follow all Transact-SQL rules for identifiers.

3. The third section allows us to enter text that describes the stored procedure. We can select Query —> Specify Values for Template Parameters, or press Ctrl + Shift + M, to display the Specify Values for Template Parameters dialog box, as shown below. where we can enter values for the parameters

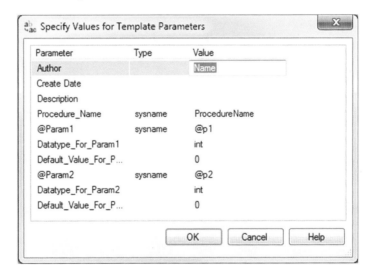

4. The fourth section is where we set the name of the stored procedure and define any parameters

5. The fifth section is where we add our SQL statements for the stored procedure

That covers the basics of creating stored procedures.

In the next section, we start developing the support code for the DataAccess layer by preparing the stored procedures for selection or execution.

Preparing the Select and Execute Methods

Unfortunately, sored procedures do not just set themselves up. To execute a stored procedure, we need to perform the following tasks:

- Open a connection to the database

- Create the SqlCommand object

- Add the stored procedures parameters

- Retrieve any Output parameters

In this section, we will develop the support code that is necessary for Coding Briefs to be able to select and execute data via stored procedures.

Setting up Stored Procedures

The first step in setting up the store procedure for Coding Briefs is to develop the SetUpSP procedure in which we will open a connection to the database, create the SqlCommand object, get a list of the stored procedure's parameters, and retrieve any Output parameters, as shown in Listing 6.

```vb
Public Sub SetUpSP(ByVal SPName As String,
  ByRef numOutParms As Object,
  Optional, ByVal parms() As Object = Nothing)
  Try
    'Open the connection.
    DBConnect(rbConn)
    'Create the Command.
    SqlCmd = New SqlCommand(SPName, SqlConn)
    SqlCmd.CommandType = CommandType.StoredProcedure
    'Get the Parameters for the Stored Procedure.
    Call RetrieveParameters(SqlCmd, numOutParms)
    'Set the number of Output Parameters.
    Dim outParms(numOutParms - 1) As Object
    ' Add the values to the Parameters.
    ' I start at 1 here because parameter 0 is the
    ' ReturnCode
    For i = 1 To SqlCmd.Parameters.Count - 1
      With SqlCmd.Parameters(i)
        ' Add the Direction and Value to the
        ' Input Parameters.
        If .Direction = ParameterDirection.Input Then
          .Value = parms(i - 1).ToString
        Else
          ' You must explicitly set the
          ' Direction of the OutPut Parameters.
          .Direction = ParameterDirection.Output
        End If
      End With
    Next
  Catch
  Catch ' Return the error to the calling program.
    errorParms(0) = 999
    errorParms(1) = Err.Description
    errorParms(2) = System.Reflection.MethodBase.
    GetCurrentMethod.Name
  End Try
End Sub
```

Listing 6: Setting up Stored Procedures

The code in Listing 6 sets up the store procedure so that it can be executed as needed.

First, we make a call to DBConnect to open the connection to the database.

Second, we create the SqlCommand object, which represents our stored procedure that will be executed against the SQL Server 2008 database.

The third section of code makes a call to the GetParameters procedure that we will develop later in this brief. The GetParameters procedure reads the parameters from a store procedure.

The next code section adds the values to the input parameters and sets the direction of the Output parameters

The Catch statement has our normal error trapping.

Note: Even though the Direction property of the Output parameters is set by the DeriveParameters method, we must explicitly set it to Output, or an error will be raised.

Working with Parameters

If we need to select data from a stored procedure based on a certain set of criteria, we can add parameters to the stored procedure. Parameters allow us to pass information to SQL Server. Once SQL Server has the information, it becomes a variable that we can use. Parameters can be used to limit the data that is returned from the select statement in the stored procedure. Parameters must be added to the Parameters object before they can be used.

Adding Stored Procedure Parameters

Parameters are part of the SQL Server SQLCommand object and they must be added to the Parameters collection before they can be used. To add a parameter to the Parameters collection, we must supply the following information:

- The name of the parameter
- The data type of the data that will be passed
- The value to be passed
- If the parameter is not an input parameter, we must supply the direction of the parameter. Valid parameter directions are:
    - ◊ Input, the default, where the parameter is an input parameter
    - ◊ InputOutput, where the parameter can perform as both an input and an output parameter
    - ◊ Output, where the parameter is an output parameter and it can return a value to the calling program
    - ◊ ReturnValue, where the parameter represents a return value

The basic code necessary to add a parameter to the Parameters collection is demonstrated below in Code 2.

```vb
' Create the command and set its properties.
Dim command As SqlCommand = New SqlCommand()
command.Connection = connection
command.CommandText = "usrVerifyUsers"
command.CommandType = CommandType.StoredProcedure

' Add the input parameter and set its properties.
Dim parameter As New SqlParameter()
parameter.ParameterName = "@UserName"
parameter.SqlDbType = SqlDbType.NVarChar
parameter.Direction = ParameterDirection.Input
parameter.Value = userName

' Add the parameter to the Parameters collection.
command.Parameters.Add(parameter)
```

Code2: Basic Parameters

We can also add the parameter in a one-line operation, as shown in Code 3.

```vb
' Create the command and set its properties.
Dim command As SqlCommand = New SqlCommand()
command.Connection = connection
command.CommandText = "usrVerifyUsers"
command.CommandType = CommandType.StoredProcedure

' Add the input parameter and set its properties.
cmd.Parameters.Add(New SqlParameter
  ("@AccountID", AccountID))
```

Code3: One Line Parameters

Having SQL Server Retrieve the Parameters

There are two basic ways to work with parameters in Visual Studio 2010:

- Add parameters to the parameter object manually, as shown in Code 2 and Code 3, the hard way

- Have SQL Server read a given stored procedure and return the parameters, the easy way

In our case, in the SetUpSP procedure that we developed in section, *Setting up Stored Procedures*, earlier in this brief, we are having SQL Server read the stored procedure and return the parameters.

Retrieving Stored Procedure Parameters

We can use the DeriveParameters method of the SQLCommandBuilder to retrieve parameter information from a stored procedure and populate the Parameters collection of the specified SqlCommand object. Using the DeriveParameters method means that we are letting SQL Server do the heavy lifting for us , as shown in Listing 7.

```vb
Public Sub RetrieveParameters(
 ByVal cmd As SqlClient.SqlCommand,
 ByRef numOutParms As Int16)

Try
   SqlCommandBuilder.DeriveParameters(cmd)

   Dim objParms As Object = Nothing
   Dim obj As SqlParameter
   For Each obj In cmd.Parameters
    If obj.Direction =
      ParameterDirection.InputOutput Then
      numOutParms += 1
    End If
   Next
 Catch
  'Show any errors
  MessageBox.Show(Err.Description & " " & _
  Me.ToString & vbNewLine & Err.Description)
 End Try
End Sub
```

Listing 7: Retrieving Parameters

The code in Listing 7 uses the DeriveParameters method to populate the parameters collection.

The first part of the code uses the DeriveParameters method to populate the parameters collection.

After the parameters are retrieved, we examine the direction of each parameter. If the direction is Output, we increment the number of Output parameters by 1. We do this so that we will know if we have any Output parameters and the number of Output parameters when we execute the stored procedure. That way, we can format any Output parameters and return them to the calling procedure. That is why we have defined the numOutParms variable as ByRef.

The Catch statement has our normal error trapping. If an error is encountered, it will be displayed to the user.

Stored procedure parameters are a little tricky to work with, but once tamed, they are very useful tools.

In the next section, we will develop the process to return any Output parameters to their calling procedure.

Note: The DeriveParameters method makes a separate call to the stored procedure, so keep that in mind as you develop data intensive applications

Returning Output Parameters

Stored procedures provide an excellent way to manipulate data. Parameters extend the functionality of stored procedures by allowing us to send information to a stored procedure in an Input parameter, and return data in the form of an Output parameter.

Output parameters are great vehicles for returning a single data value, such as the Identity of the record that is added, or the result of a computation, or any other data that we want to return in addition to the normal data that is in the Select statement or the ReturnCode.

Retrieving Output Parameters

Output parameters allow us to return specific data in addition to the data that is returned in our Select statement or the ReturnCode. In this brief, we manage the Output parameters in the SetOutParms procedure that is called from the select and execute procedures, as shown in Listing 8.

```vbnet
Private Function SetOutParms( _
  ByRef parms As Object(),
  ByVal numOutParms As Int16,
  ByRef errorParms As Object) As Int16

  Dim i As Int16 = 0
  Dim j As Int16 = 0

  Try
    'Redim the parmObject to the number of
    OutPut Parameters so that we can return
      them to the calling routine.
    ReDim parms(numOutParms - 1)


    'Add the value of the OutPut Parameters to
    the parmObject.
    For i = 1 To SqlCmd.Parameters.Count - 1
     With SqlCmd.Parameters(i)
       If .Direction <>
          ParameterDirection.Input Then
         parms(j) = .Value.ToString
         j += 1
       End If
     End With
    Next
    Return i
    Catch
      ' Return the error to the calling
        program.
    errorParms(0) = 999
    errorParms(1) = Err.Description
    errorParms(2) = System.
      Reflection.MethodBase.
    GetCurrentMethod.Name
   End Try
   Return i
End Function
```

Listing 8: Setting Output Parameters

The code in Listing 8 formats the Output parameters so that they can be returned to the calling procedure.

First, we reset the parms object to the number of Output parameters, so that the parms object will be ready to be returned to the calling procedure.

Second, we loop through the parameters collection looking for the Output parameters. When we find one, we add it to the parms object to be returned to the calling procedure.

The Catch statement has our normal error trapping.

That completes the development of the Coding Briefs' Data Access Layer. It is now ready to be used, but before we dive into the sample projects, we need to get that paperwork out of the way. In the next section, we will document all of the function calls that are exposed by the data access framework.

Documenting the Data Access Layer

The data access layer that we have developed in this Coding Brief can be used for Windows applications and ASP .Net Web sites. It includes the following function calls:

- DBConnect
- DBCreateDataset
- DBDisconnect
- DBExecNonQuery
- DBGetSqlDataReader
- RetrieveParameters
- SetOutParms
- SetUpSP

Let's take a closer look at each of the functions in the DAL.

DBConnect(String, ref Object[])
Make a connection to the database.

Syntax
```
Public Sub DBConnect(
connectionString As String,
errorParms As Object())
```

Parameters

Name	Type	Description
connectionString	String	Database Connection String
errorParms	Object	Holds any Errors

Remarks
Internal call

DBCreateDataset(String, String, ref Object[], ref Object[])
Creates a Dataset from a Stored Procedure and returns it to the calling program.

Syntax
```
Public Function DBCreateDataset(
    SPName As String,    cbConn As
String, errorParms As Object(),
    parms As Object()) As DataSet
```

Parameters

Name	Type	Description
SPName	String	Stored procedure name
cbConn	String	the connection string
errorParms	Object	Holds the errors
parms	Object	The parameters for the stored procedure

Returns   Remarks
a Dataset   parms are optional

24

DBDisconnect(ref Object)

Close the connection to the database.

Syntax
```
Public Sub DBDisconnect(
    errorParms As Object)
```

Parameters

Name	Type	Description
errorParms	Object	Holds the errors

Remarks
Internal call

DBExecNonQuery(String, String, ref Object, ref Object[])

Executes a Stored Procedure against the connection and returns the number of rows affected.

Syntax
```
Public Function DBExecNonQuery(
    spName As String, cbConn As String,
    errorParms As Object,
    parms As Object()) As Int
```

Parameters

Name	Type	Description
spName	String	The name of the stored procedure
cbConn	String	The connection string
errorParms	Object	Holds any errors
parms	Object	Parameters for the stored procedure

Returns
The number of rows affected

Remarks
parms are optional

DBGetSqlDataReader(String, String, ref Object[], ref Object[])

Creates a SqlDataReader from a Stored Procedure and returns it to the calling program.

Syntax
```
Public Function DBGetSqlDataReader(
    spName As String,cbConn As String,
    errorParms As Object(),parms
    As Object()) As SqlDataReader
```

Parameters

Name	Type	Description
spName	String	The name of the stored procedure
cbConn	String	The connection string
errorParms	Object	Holds any errors
parms	Object	Parameters for the stored procedure

Returns
a SQL DataReader

Remarks
parms are optional

RetrieveParameters (SqlCommand, ref Int16, Object[])

Read the parameters from the Stored Procedure and add them to the SQLCommand Object.

Syntax
```
Public Sub RetrieveParameters(cmd As
    SqlCommand, numOutParms As Short,
    errorParms As Object())
```

Parameters

Name	Type	Description
cmd	SqlCommand	The command object
numOutParms	Int16	The number of output parameters
errorParms	Object	Holds any errors

Remarks
Internal call

SetOutParms(ref Object[], Int16, ref Object)

Set up the Output parms to be returned to the calling program.

Syntax

```
Private Function SetOutParms(parms As
   Object(),numOutParms As Short,
   errorParms As Object) As Short
```

Parameters

Name	Type	Description
parms	Object	The parameters for the stored procedure
numOutParms	Int16	The number of output parameters
errorParms	Object	Holds any errors

Returns

The number of output parameters

Remarks

Internal call

SetUpSP(String, ref Object, String, ref Object[], Object[])

Open the connection, create the Command, and add values to the parameters.

Syntax

```
Public Sub SetUpSP(SPName As String,
   numOutParms As Object,   cbConn As
   String,errorParms As Object(),
   parms As Object())
```

Parameters

Name	Type	Description
SPName	String	The name of the stored procedure
numOutParms	Object	The number of output parameters
cbConn	String	The connection string
errorParms	Object	Holds any errors
parms	Object	Parameters for the stored procedure

Remarks

parms are optional, internal call

So, there we have it, a completely documented Data Access Framework. Now, the only thing left to do is take it for a test run. And we are in luck! This volume of Coding Briefs includes two sample projects: a test project for Windows applications: and a test Web site. So, stay tuned, the fun is about to begin!

In the next section, we'll get started with an overview of the sample projects.

Defining the Sample Projects

As mentioned earlier, this volume of Coding Briefs includes two sample projects that will take advantage of the Data Access Framework we have developed. One is a Windows forms application, and the other is in ASP .Net. Both of these projects will select, insert, update, and delete records from a Contacts database. Let's get started by attaching the Contacts database.

Attaching the Contact Database

The Contacts database is located in the project files of the Database folder. Follow these steps to attach the database to SQL Server 2008:

1. Open SQL Server Management Studio

2. Right mouse click on the Database folder and select Attach from the menu to display the Attach Databases dialog box, as shown below

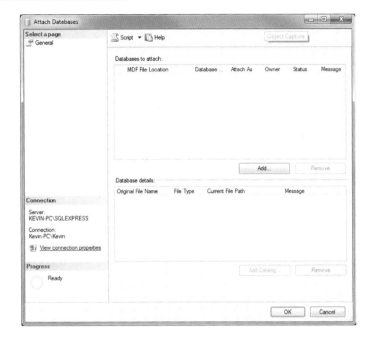

3. Click the Add button and navigate to the CodingBasics.mdf file and select it

4. Click the OK button on the Locate Database Files dialog box to select the Contacts database

5. Click the Add button on the Attach Databases dialog box to attach the CodingBriefs database

The CodingBriefs database includes one table named Contacts, as shown below in Figure 6, and four stored procedures that are listed in Table 3.

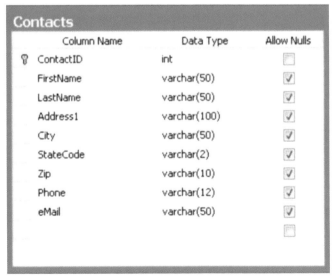

Figure 6: The Contacts Database

Table 3: Data Access Stored Procedures

Stored Procedure Name	Description
delContacts	Deletes a contact
insContacts	Inserts a new contact
selAllContacts	Selects all of the records from the Contacts table
updZip	Updates the Zip Code for a selected contact record

Now that we have the database attached, it is time to investigate the Windows sample application.

Investigating the Windows Sample Application

The Windows sample application (WSA), as shown in Figure 7, and the ASP .Net sample application (ASA), as shown in Figure 9, are designed to allow the user to select, update, insert, and delete records from the Contacts database.

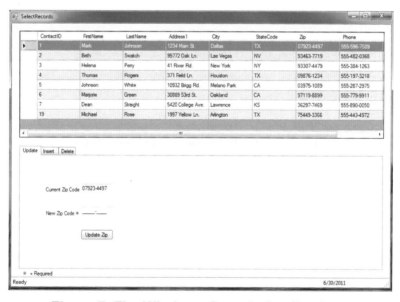

Figure 7: The Windows Sample Application

The WSA has a DataGridView control on the top of the form that lists all of the records in the Contacts database. The Tab control at the bottom of the form holds the Update, Insert, and Delete functionality that allows the user to update, insert, and delete records from the database.

Defining the Tiers

Our sample applications, the Windows Sample application (WSA), and the AST .Net (ASA), are both excellent examples of 3-tiered architecture, consisting of the following tiers:

- a UI Tier that is comprised of the forms

- a Business Object Tier that holds the business objects and the business rules

- a Data tier that is the Contacts database

The tiers work in concert to provide a well-formed, robust developmental foundation that can be used as a model for future projects.

Trapping Errors in the Code

The WSA sample application includes a complete error trapping system that monitors all of the functions and procedures in customized Try/Catch statements. If an error is encountered any-where in the WSA, a MessageBox will be displayed to the user that lets him or her know the description and location of the error in the code base.

Maintaining Data Integrity

Data integrity is a very important aspect of any data-driven application. For our purposes in this Coding Brief, a data validation region has been added to the code that is responsible for maintaining data integrity. The data formats are defined in the Validating events of the data entry code, and if a data entry error is encountered, a standard Error Provider is displayed to alert the user of the error. This is accomplished in a custom data validation routine that can be incorporated in all of our applications and used to validate controls on all of our forms.

Now that we have a good idea of the WAS, let's jump right in and get it up and running.

Running the Windows Sample Application

The WSA is included in the project files that can be downloaded from www.runtimepublishing.com. Follow these steps to get the WSA up and running:

1. Follow the steps in the section, *Quick Start,* to register and unlock the code for this Coding Brief

2. The unlock Code is **1210-1045-9482-9641-9701**

3. Open the CodingBriefVolume1 project in Visual Studio 2010. The CBDataAccess project has already been added to the solution.

That is all there is to it.

> **Note:** The CBDataAccess project is developed as a dll. The reason that we are adding the project here and not just a reference to the dll is that we want to be able to debug and follow the code in the CBDataAccess project. For production applications, all that has to be done is to add a reference to the CBDataAccess dll.

Calling the Data Access Framework

We have been developing the data access framework throughout this Coding Brief, and it is time to put it to use. The first section of code that we will discuss is the code to select records, but before we do that, it is important for us to go over the strategy of using a Business Object tier.

Working with Business Objects

The Business Object tier manages all of the business rules in the data access framework. In a well-defined data access framework, it is very important to separate the tiers. With the tiers separated, it makes it much easier to interchange database engines and UI.

Now, finally, let's get down to the fun part and run some code!

Selecting Records

Follow these steps as we investigate the Data Access Framework and select records from the Contacts table:

1. Open the code window for the Select form to show the Codebehind

2. Locate the following line of code in the Form_Load procedure and notice a bookmark on the following line of code

   ```
   Call Me.SelectAllRecords()
   ```

3. Press F5 to run the project and follow the flow and see the call to the DAF

We will see the code go through the Select form, then to the Business Object, and to the DAF. Finally, the process will return to the Select form and populate the DataViewGrid.

The process to select records is fairly straight forward. Next, we will spice things up a bit as we start with, what we will call, the Action Buttons, as we update a Contact record's Zip Code.

Updating the Zip Code

Follow along with these steps as we use the Update Zip button on the Update tab to perform some magic and update the contact's zip code:

1. Open the Select form
2. Double click on the Update Zip button to display the code for the Click event
3. Notice the break point on the line of code that makes a call to the Business Object

   ```
   success = execBO.UpdateZip(curID, slParms(0), My.Settings.cbConn,
       errorParms)
   ```

4. Press F5 to start the application
5. Select a record from the DataGridView
6. Enter a new Zip code
7. Click the Update Zip Button and follow along as the code goes through the Business Object and the DAF, and finally returns to the Select form

As demonstrated in this section, updating records is like child's play if we use a data access framework to do all of the hard work for us. .

Now, we will insert a new record into the Contacts table.

Inserting a new Contact

Follow these steps to add a new contact and see the code in action:

1. Open the Select form
2. Double click on the Insert New Contact button to display the code for the Click event
3. Notice the break point on the line of code that makes a call to the Business Object

```
success = execBO.InsertContact(
    slParms,
    My.Settings.cbConn,
    errorParms)
```

4. Press F5 to start the application
5. Select the Insert tab
6. Enter values for the new contact fields
7. Click the Insert New Contact button and follow along as the code goes through the Business Object and the DAF, and finally returns to the Select form

Inserting new records into a database table is quick and easy if we have a well-developed data access framework in place.

Now, we will delete a record from the Contacts table.

Deleting a Contact

Follow these steps to delete a contact from the database and see the code in action:

1. Open the Select form
2. Double click on the Delete Contact button to display the code for the Click event
3. Notice the break point on the line of code that makes a call to the Business Object

```
success = execBO.DeleteContact(
    slParms,
    My.Settings.cbConn,
    errorParms)
```

4. Press F5 to start the application
5. Select the Delete tab
6. Select a contact from the DataGridView to be deleted
7. Click the Delete Contact button and follow along as the code goes through the Business Object and the DAF, and finally returns to the Select form

Having the ability to delete records is necessary to keep a database current, and with the help of our data access framework, it is an easy task.

That completes our Windows Sample Application walk-through; however, spending some additional time working with the sample application, as well as checking out the other sections, is certainly encouraged.

In the final section of this Coding Brief, we will take a quick look at the ASP. Net Sample Application (ASA) .

What's Happening in the ASP. Net Sample Application?

The ASA includes all of the functionality of the WAS, but is it tweaked for the Web. We will discuss the major differences in the next sections.

Trapping Errors in the Code

A complete error trapping system that monitors all of the functions and procedures in our customized Try/Catch statements has been included, but there are some changes in the ASP .NET version. The most important change is the use of Alert boxes, as shown below in Figure 8, instead of MessageBoxes.

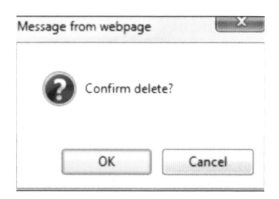

If an error is encountered anywhere in the ASA, an Alert box will be displayed to the user that lets him or her know the description of the error and the location of the error in the code base. Since it is difficult to display an Alert box on the fly from within a Class or a Module, if an error is encountered, the error will be returned to the ASPX page where it can be easily displayed.

Maintaining Data Integrity

Data integrity in ASP .NET applications can be managed with a group of Validation controls that are included in Visual Studio 2010. For the ASA, we will rely on the RequiredFieldValidation, RegularExpressionValidation, and ValidationSummary controls to maintain the integrity of the data that is entered. Figure 9, shows the Validation controls in action.

CODING BRIEFS V1 DATA ACCESS FRAMEWORK

Update   Insert   Delete

	ContactID	FirstName	LastName	Address1	City	StateCode	Zip
Select	1	Mark	Johnson	1234 Main St.	Dallas	TX	07923-4497
Select	2	Beth	Swatch	95772 Oak Ln.	Las Vegas	NV	93463-7719
Select	3	Helena	Perry	41 River Rd.	New York	NY	93307-4479
Select	4	Thomas	Rogers	371 Field Ln.	Houston	TX	09876-1234
Select	5	Johnson	White	10932 Brigg Rd.	Melano Park	CA	03975-1089
Select	6	Marjorie	Green	30889 53rd St.	Oakland	CA	97119-8899
Select	7	Dean	Straight	5420 College Ave.	Lawrence	KS	36297-7469
Select	19	Michael	Rose	1997 Yellow Ln.	Arlington	TX	75449-3366

UPDATE

Current Zip Code   07923-4497

New Zip Code   *

[Update the Contact]

Figure 9: Validation Controls

Controlling the Views

Another difference between our Windows Sample Application and our ASPX Sample Application is the way that we manage what the user views. In the WSA, a Tab control has been used to keep all of the functionality separated. ASP .Net does not have a Tab control, so we have relied on a MultiView control with separate View controls to segregate the functionality. The current view is set in separate ASPX pages for insert, update, and delete actions.

Views are containers that are displayed in a ContentView Control, as shown in Figure 10. Views can hold other controls, such as Textboxes, Labels, and Images. View controls can be thought of as the pages of a Tab control. Controls can be added to the Views in design mode. At runtime, we can set the View that is shown. The other Views are invisible until we set a different View to be the Current View.

The following code can be used to set the Current View that is seen by the user:

```
' Set DefaultView as the active view.
ContactsMultiView.SetActiveView(UpdateView)
```

In this case, UpdateView is the name of one of the Views. We can have as many Views as we need, but only one View can be shown at a time. Figure 10 shows the Views in the ASP .Net Sample Application.

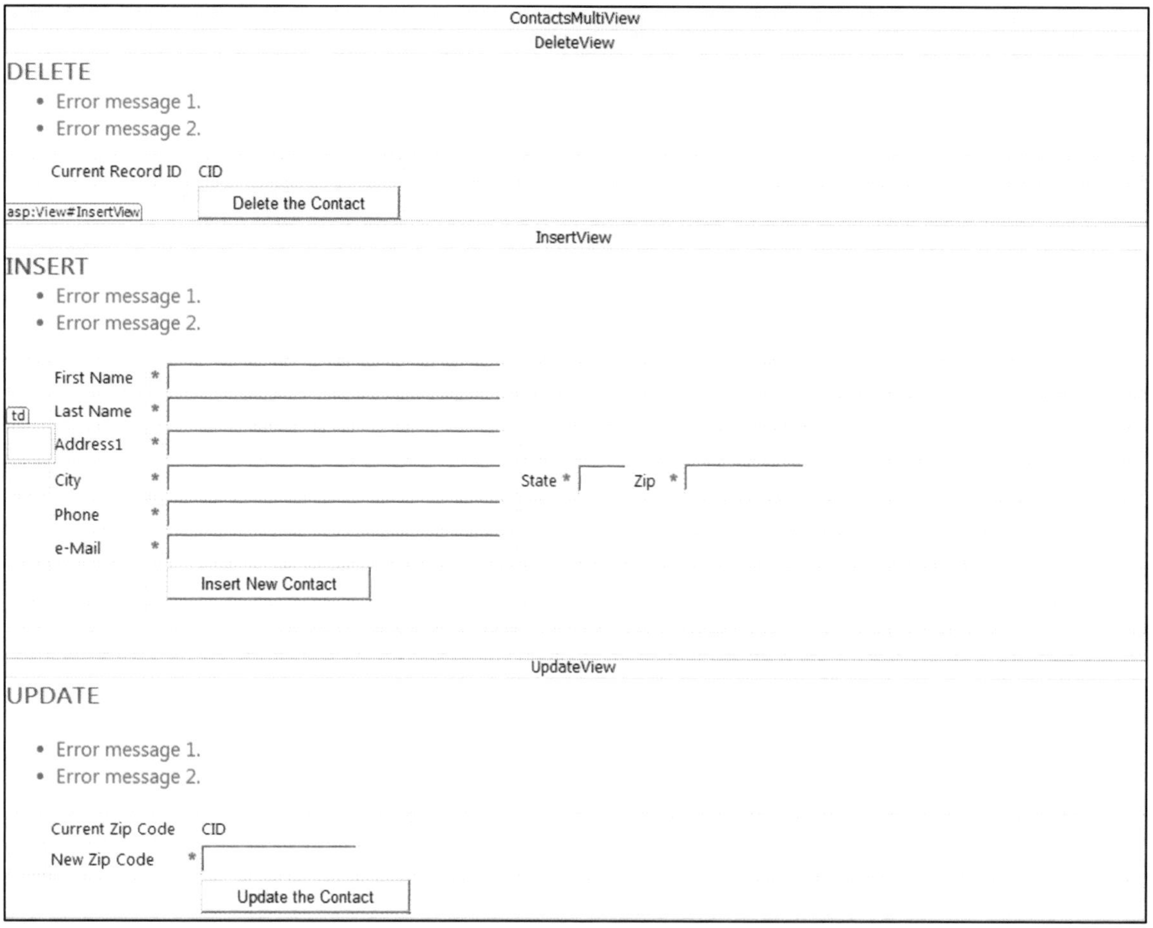

Figure 10: Views

Using Master Pages

In Visual Studio 2010, when a new ASP .NET Web Application project is created, the default project comes complete with a Master Page. To make the development of the ASP sample more robust, we have kept the default Master Page, and developed from there.

Running the ASP .Net Sample Application

The ASP .Net Sample Application is included in the project files that can be downloaded from www.runtimepublishing.com. Follow these steps to get the ASA up and running:

1. Follow the steps in the section, *Quick Start,* to register and unlock the code for this Coding Brief if not done already

2. Open the CodingBriefVolume1Web project in Visual Studio 2010. The solution already includes the CBDataAccess project

Since the calls to the data access framework and the Business Objects are the same in our ASP. Net sample application as they are in our Windows Sample Application, we will not go through the ASA. However, several bookmarks have been added to help get us going, and there are lots of best practices in the code to get us thinking. Now, it's time to give it a try, and have some fun!

The ASP .NET Sample Application is set up and ready to run.

> **Note:** The CBDataAccess project is developed as a dll. The reason that we are adding the project here and not just a reference to the dll is that we want to be able to debug and follow the code in the CBDataAccess project. For production applications, all we have to do is to add a reference to the CBDataAccess dll.

Contacting Us

You can use any of the following ways to contact Runtime Publishing, LLC:

By mail:

14096 Preston Rd, Suite 404-505

Dallas, TX, USA 75345

E-mail: support@runtimepublisning.com

Web site: www.runtimepublishing.com

Made in the USA
Charleston, SC
28 July 2011